The Main I

presen

Mildred Smith's Favourite Family Recipes

in association with

GRANADA
TELEVISION

Published by Sigma Leisure - an imprint of
Sigma Press, 1 South Oak Lane, Wilmslow, Cheshire SK9 6AR, England.

British Library Cataloguing in Publication Data
A CIP record for this book is available from the British Library.

ISBN: 1-85058-555-5

Editorial, typesetting and page design by: Sigma Press, Wilmslow, Cheshire.

Cover design and printing: MFP Design & Print

Cover photographs: main picture – Mildred Smith *(Mike Frisbee)* and *The Main Ingredient* reporter, Mark Owen, and presenter, Lucy Meacock *(Granada Television Ltd)*

Illustrations: Victoria Bentley Smith

Executive Producer for *The Main Ingredient*: Mike Spencer

Producer for *The Main Ingredient*: Debbie Pollitt

Preface

We've had two successful series of Granada Television's The Main Ingredient now, in both of which I've had the pleasure of participating. And last year, I was overwhelmed at the wonderful response to my first Main Ingredient recipe book. I'm so pleased people have enjoyed the recipes so far and I hope that with this new book, and with the third television series in the new year, people will continue to sample and savour my favourite food.

Food's always been a big part of my life and, as you'll find when you read on, there's often a story to tell – after all, you can't cook for 50 years without accumulating some culinary tales, can you?

So, read on, eat on and enjoy – you deserve a treat!

Mildred Smith

Healthy Eating Note!

Mildred Smith uses traditional ingredients in these recipes. In most cases, lard and butter can be substituted by mono- or polyunsaturated margarines. Where frying is involved, vegetable oil can be used. These changes will reduce the intake of saturated fats in line with current dietary opinion.

Metrication!

Quantities in the recipes are given in both Imperial (which Mildred and other traditional cooks still use) and metric. For the best results, use one or the other – do not mix the Imperial and metric quantities.

Contents

Soups

"Soup of the evening, beautiful soup"...so pronounced the Mock Turtle in Alice's Adventures in Wonderland – and he's not the only one who loves it. So when you've got time to abandon the packets and the cans, why not make your own – there's nothing tastier with a slice of crusty bread."

First Things First – in the soup!

My first encounter with a pan of soup was many years ago in the school kitchen. Another girl and I were told to clean some shelves right near the cooker where cook was making soup for lunch. Everything was going well...until, by accident, we knocked a can of cleaning powder off the shelves and – yes, you've guessed it – right, smack into the pan of simmering soup! We stood petrified for a moment. "Perhaps if we stir it up, it'll be alright"said my friend hopefully. We did. It tasted awful (what a surprise!) and we were obliged to own up.

Basic soup-making

Most soups can be made very easily, particularly if you own a blender. Clean and cut your chosen vegetable into small pieces. Fry gently, in butter or margarine, until softened. Add your stock, or in the case of cream soups, your milk and water, or cream, then cook until the vegetables are completely soft. If you have a blender, liquidise the mixture; return to the pan, season, and add any finishing touches.

Cream of Tomato Soup

"You'll never buy another tin after you've tasted my tomato soup. It's just the job for a winter warmer!"

Ingredients

4 – 6 servings

1 lb (450 g) ripe tomatoes, skinned and quartered
½ onion, coarsely chopped
4 oz (110 g) carrot, peeled and chopped
1 bouquet garni sachet
2 tbsp tomato puree
2 pints (1.1 litres) chicken or vegetable stock
Salt and pepper
¼ pint (150 ml) single cream

Method

Put the tomatoes, onion, carrot, bouquet garni, tomato puree, and stock into a pan. Bring slowly to the boil, cover and simmer for 30 minutes. Remove the bouquet garni, and allow soup to cool slightly. Liquidise the soup, in a food processor, or with a blender, until smooth. Return to the pan and season to taste. Heat gently, stirring in the cream. Sprinkle with chopped parsley or chives as liked. Serve with fresh bread, or croutons.

Croutons

Cut the crusts from slices of bread and cut into four triangles. If slices are large, cut into half again. Fry in hot vegetable or sunflower oil until golden-brown. If you like garlic, add a little to the oil for extra flavour. Croutons will keep for two to three weeks if stored in an air-tight container, and kept in a cool place.

Spicy Carrot Soup

"Whoever heard of spicy soup? Well this one should 'cumin' handy."

Ingredients

4 – 6 servings

1½ lb (675 g) carrots, peeled and chopped
1 onion, peeled and chopped
I clove garlic, peeled and crushed
2 tsp ground coriander
1 tsp ground cumin
1½ pints (850 ml) of chicken or vegetable stock
½ pint (300 ml) milk (half-fat if preferred)
2 oz (50 g) butter or margarine
Salt and black pepper

Method

Heat the butter or margarine in a large frying-pan. Add the onion and carrots, toss to cover, and fry gently for 10 minutes.

Add the spices and garlic and fry for 1 minute. Pour on the stock, add the seasoning, and bring to the boil, stirring frequently. Cover and simmer for 30 minutes, stirring occasionally.

Allow to cool a little, then liquidise until smooth. Return to the pan and add milk. Reheat gently, and serve with croutons (see page 5).

Butterbean and Onion Soup

"Soups aren't just for starters. Try this one with some fresh crusty bread – it's a meal in itself!"

Ingredients

Serves 4

   1 lb (450 g) onions, thinly sliced
   15 oz (420 g) can of butter beans (drained)
   1½ pints (850 ml) vegetable stock
   ¼ pint (150 ml) of single cream
   2 tsp caster sugar
   3 tbsp oil
   1 tbsp chives, snipped
   Salt and black pepper

Method

Heat the oil in a saucepan, add the onions, cover and cook gently until soft.

   Add the stock and beans, cover and simmer for 20 minutes.

   Sprinkle in the sugar, and cook for a further 2 minutes. Liquidise the soup until smooth, return to rinsed-out pan, stir in the cream, chives and season to taste. Heat through without boiling, and serve garnished with a few more chives, or parsley as liked.

Bacon and Lentil Soup

"Be rasher than ever and bung in the bacon for a soup that's sure to satisfy."

Ingredients

Serves 4

> 2 onions, peeled and chopped
> 4 rashers of middle bacon (unsmoked), derinded and cut into small pieces.
> 1 large potato, peeled and diced
> 4 oz (110 g) red lentils
> 1½ pints (850 ml) of stock, preferably vegetable
> 1 tbsp tomato puree
> 1 tsp oregano (dried)
> 1 tbsp parsley, chopped
> Black pepper (fresh ground if possible)

Method

In a large saucepan, fry the bacon and onions with as little fat as possible.

Add the potato and lentils and cook for 4-5 minutes. Add the stock, tomato puree, oregano and pepper, bring to the boil, then cover and simmer for 40 minutes. Remove the lid, and simmer for about 10 minutes until the soup thickens slightly. Stir in the parsley, and serve.

Mushroom Soup

"A good friend of mine always says, 'the problem with your mushroom soup, Mildred, is if you eat too much of it, there's not mush-room for anything else!' 'Eat your soup' I always answer with a smile."

Ingredients

Serves 4

8 oz (225 g) of mushrooms, wiped
2 oz (50 g) of butter
12 fl oz (330 ml) milk, approx
1 tbsp plain flour
Salt and pepper
4 tbsp single cream

Method

Keep two small mushrooms aside, and slice thinly for garnish. Slice the rest and cook with half the butter in a covered pan for about 10 minutes, or until tender. Liquidise or sieve, leaving them a little coarse as this makes for a nice texture.

Strain the juice from the pan, add the milk and make up to three-quarters of a pint.

Melt the remaining butter in the pan, stir in the flour, and add the liquid gradually, stirring, until it is smooth and thick.

Add the mushrooms, season, bring to the boil, then reduce the heat, and simmer for 2-3 minutes. Pour into serving bowls, add a tablespoon of cream to each – give it a swirl for a marbled effect. Garnish with the sliced mushrooms.

Note: To make the soup even more delicious, substitute half the milk for single cream.

Celery Soup

"This is so easy, but really delicious. Stick to celery for a simple soup and a scrumptious supper."

Ingredients

Serves 4

1 head of celery
1 oz (25 g) of margarine or butter
1 oz (25 g) of flour
12 fl oz (330 g) pint milk
Salt and pepper

Method

Wash the celery and cut into small pieces. Put in a large saucepan with just enough water (add a little milk to this) to cover. Add a pinch of salt and cook until soft. Sieve or liquidise to make a puree.

Melt the butter in a pan, stir in the flour, and add the milk gradually. When smooth and thick, add the pureed celery, heat through and season to taste.

Cucumber Soup

"Forget about afternoon tea on the vicarage lawn. Hot or cold, cucumber makes a classy soup."

Ingredients

Serves 4 – 6

1 large cucumber
4 oz (110 g) margarine
2 small onions
2 pints (1.1 litres) boiling water
1 egg yolk
Salt, pepper, nutmeg and cayenne pepper (to taste)
1 tbsp double cream

Method

Peel and thinly slice the cucumber. Fry gently in 1 oz (25 g) of the margarine for 2-3 minutes. Fry the sliced onions in the remaining margarine.

Put the onions and cucumber into a saucepan, add the boiling water, season and simmer for 30 minutes. Liquidise. Just before serving, mix the beaten egg yolk and cream together, add a tablespoon of the hot soup to them, take the pan of soup off the heat and add the cream mixture, stirring thoroughly. **Do not allow to boil** or the egg will curdle. Serve with croutons (see page 5).

This soup may be chilled and served cold, if preferred.

Watercress Soup

"When I was a girl, watercress grew in the local streams. Nowadays, we buy it at the local shop, but it still makes a lovely soup with a wonderful colour."

Ingredients

Serves 4

1 large or two small bunches of watercress
1 large onion, peeled and finely chopped
1 large potato, peeled and diced
1 pint (570 ml) chicken or vegetable stock
10 fl oz (275 ml) milk
1 tbsp oil
Black pepper

Method

Heat the oil in a pan, and fry the onion gently for 5 minutes.

Add the diced potato, and cook for 5 more minutes. Liquidise the watercress (or chop finely) into stock. Add to the onion and potato and bring to the boil. Cover and simmer for 30 minutes. Liquidise until smooth, add the milk and reheat gently.

This soup can be served hot or cold.

Vegetable (Cream) Soup

"This creamy concoction's just the job for the various vegetables left in the fridge – go on, give 'em a tasty treat!"

Ingredients

Serves 4 – 6

1½ lb (675 g) of mixed vegetables, (carrots, onion, potatoes, green peas, turnip etc) prepared by cleaning and dicing.
1½ oz (40 g) butter or margarine
1½ pints (850 ml) vegetable stock or water
10 fl oz (275 ml) milk
2 tbsp flour
1 tbsp chopped parsley
Salt and pepper

Method

Melt the fat in a saucepan, and add vegetables. Fry over a moderate heat for 5-6 minutes stirring. Cover the pan, and cook for 10 minutes, shaking to prevent sticking. Add the stock, season to taste, and cook until vegetables are tender. Blend the flour with a little milk until smooth. Add to the pan and cook for 5 minutes. Remove the soup, liquidise, return to the pan and add the remaining milk and parsley. Bring slowly to the boil, then remove and serve.

Cauliflower Soup

"We all grew cauliflowers in our vegetable patch – and the family enjoyed this as an alternative to cauliflower cheese."

Ingredients

Serves 4 – 6

1 small cauliflower
1 small onion
Sprig of parsley
$\frac{1}{2}$ oz (15 g) margarine
Pinch of ground mace or nutmeg
$1\frac{1}{2}$ pints (850 ml) of vegetable stock
1 pint (570 ml) milk
$1\frac{1}{2}$ tsp cornflour
Seasoning

Method

Wash the cauliflower, and cut into small pieces. Peel and slice the onion. Place the onion, margarine, parsley, mace and seasoning in a pan, add the stock, bring to the boil, and simmer for 20 minutes. Add the cauliflower, and simmer for 20 more minutes. Blend the milk and cornflour, add to the soup and stir until the mixture thickens. Liquidise and reheat.

To turn this into Cheese soup, see the recipe on the following page.

Cheese Soup

Ingredients

Serves 4 – 6

2 – 4 oz (50 – 100 g) of Stilton or Danish Blue, crumbled.

Method

Make the soup as on the preceding page, and then add the crumbled cheese, after adding the milk and cornflour.

Sauces

"But Mildred, sauces are too difficult – I never get them right!"

So many people have said this to me over the years. Let me sort this out once and for all. Basic sauce making is simple once you know the foundation recipes. Exceptions aside, most sauces fall into two categories – white or brown. Successful sauce-making just needs one Main Ingredient – confidence.

Basic Recipe for White Sauce

Ingredients

1 oz (25 g) flour
1 oz (25 g) butter or margarine
10 fl oz (275 ml) milk
Salt and pepper to taste
A squeeze of lemon juice.

Method

Melt the fat in a small pan. Stir in the flour, preferably with a wooden spoon, and wait until it bubbles. Draw the pan off the heat, and add a little milk, stirring until smooth. Add the rest of the milk gradually, stirring all the time. Bring gently to the boil, boil for 2-3 minutes, then season or make additions, for example:

Parsley Sauce

Add 2 tbsps chopped parsley.

Cheese Sauce

Add 2 oz (50 g) of grated cheese, plus a pinch of dry mustard.

Egg Sauce

Add a hard-boiled egg, chopped very finely.

Dutch Sauce

Add a beaten egg yolk after the sauce has boiled.

Celery Sauce

Cook 2 sticks of celery in boiling water, until soft. Chop finely and add after boiling.

Mustard Sauce

Add 1 tbsp of ready-mixed mustard.

Onion Sauce

Cook a large onion until soft, chop and add.

Soubise Sauce

Cook as onion sauce, but rub the cooked onion through a sieve before adding and add 1 tbsp of double cream.

Bechamel Sauce

Before adding the milk to the sauce, add to it a slice of carrot, a slice of turnip, a small onion, and a bay leaf. Stew for half an hour, discard the vegetables, then add as before.

Sweet Sauces

Leave out the salt and pepper. Instead add 1 tbsp caster sugar, and 1 teaspoon Vanilla essence (or, if you have one, a Vanilla pod).

Lemon Sauce

Add the juice and grated rind of a lemon.

Custard Sauce

Add a beaten egg to 1 tbsp of caster sugar, heat the milk and pour gently over, stirring. Heat slowly until the mixture thickens.

Jam Sauce

1 tbsp jam
1 tbsp sugar
Juice of ½ lemon
5 fl oz (150 ml) water

Method

Boil all together, strain and serve.

Basic Recipe for Brown Sauce

Ingredients

2 oz (50 g) flour
2 oz (50 g) butter or margarine
10 fl oz (275 ml) of brown stock (can be made from a
    stock cube)
1 onion
1 tomato
1 slice of carrot
Pinch of mixed herbs
Salt and pepper

Method

Melt the fat in a small pan, add the chopped onion and carrot, and fry until browned. Add the flour, stir well and cook for two minutes. Add the chopped tomato, draw the pan off the heat and gradually add the stock and herbs. Stir well, bring to the boil, then turn down and simmer for about half an hour. Strain and season.

Sauce Madere

Add a tablespoon of dry sherry, and squeeze of lemon juice.

Spanish Sauce

Add two finely chopped mushrooms, and a tablespoon of sherry.

Piquant Sauce

Add a finely chopped gherkin, 1 teaspoon chopped capers, and 1 dessertspoon vinegar.

Curry Sauce

Peel and chop a small onion and a small cooking apple. Fry in 1 oz (25 g) margarine until light brown. Stir in 1 oz (25 g) flour and 1 dessertspoon curry powder. Cook for 5 minutes. Draw off the heat, add a quartered tomato and 10 fl oz (275 ml) stock. Bring to the boil, then simmer for 10 minutes, add salt, pepper and squeeze of lemon juice. Just before serving, add 1 tablespoonful sultanas.

Tomato Sauce

Ingredients

½ lb (225 g) tomatoes, skinned and chopped coarsely
Small onion, peeled and chopped
Slice of carrot
Slice of turnip
1 oz (25 g) margarine
1 teaspoon cornflour, mixed with a little milk
Pinch of sugar
salt and pepper

Method

Add enough water to cover, bring to the boil and simmer for 30 minutes. Mix a teaspoonful of cornflour with a little milk, add to the sauce with 1 oz (25 g) margarine, a pinch of sugar, salt and pepper. Stir until it thickens.

Bread Sauce

Ingredients

2 oz (50 g) breadcrumbs
Small onion, stuck with 1 clove
10 fl oz (275 ml) milk
1 oz (25 g) butter or margarine
Salt and pepper

Method

Simmer the onion in the milk for ¼ hour. Strain and pour over the breadcrumbs. Leave to soak for ½ hour. Season, reheat, and beat in the margarine.

Main Dishes

"People often ask me 'Mildred, how is it that your food always turns out so well?' 'It's practise and experience,' I usually say, always flattered by the compliment. But things haven't always gone so smoothly... and people haven't always been so grateful."

As a girl, I once attempted a rather ambitious dish for lunch. A family friend had been invited and, just as I served up the meal, our friend suggested we gave thanks for what we were about to receive. 'No!' said my mother firmly, "Let's try it first and if we're still alive afterwards, we'll thank the Almighty then!"

Roast Beef and Yorkshire Pudding

"Oh, The roast beef of England,
And old England's roast beef."

(from The Grub Street Opera by Henry Fielding)

"This is still the most identifiably English meal and the one tourists long to try. Nothing else conjures up the image of family life as well as Roast Beef and Yorkshire Pudding. Here's my recipe for a great family lunch."

Ingredients

Joint of beef, preferably top side or sirloin, and if possible, not less than 2½ lb (1.1 kg) in weight. (Smaller joints do not roast so well and tend to dry).

For the batter:

4 oz (110 g) self-raising flour
Pinch of salt
1 egg
10 fl oz (275 g) milk

Method

Make the batter first, as it should stand for at least an hour in a cool place. Sieve the flour and salt into a bowl, add the egg, and draw the flour from round the sides, beating well. Add the milk, and beat thoroughly. Wipe the meat, and sprinkle with salt and pepper. Dot about 2 oz (50 g) of lard or dripping on top, if there is little fat on the joint. Stand the joint on a rack or trivet in a roasting tin, and place in a hot oven. Gas 7, 220°C, 425°F and roast for 20 minutes. Reduce the heat to Gas 5, 190°C, 375°F and continue to cook for:

16 minutes to the pound – Rare

22 minutes to the pound – Medium

25 to 30 minutes to the pound – Well Done

During the cooking, turn and baste with the fat two or three times. Test with a fork – when juice runs clear, it is cooked. Since tastes differ, I cannot give an exact time and you must judge for yourself.

When the joint is cooked to your satisfaction, take it out of the oven, and let it stand before carving. Now turn up the over heat to Gas 7 220°C, 425°F. Put your tin or tins, each with a little fat in them into the oven, and allow to get smoking hot. Give your batter a final stir, adding two tablespoons cold water.

Pour the batter into the tin or tins, and cook for about 20 minutes.

Notes: for the best results:

- ✓ the oven and fat must be very hot
- ✓ the batter must be very cold
- ✓ don't open the oven part-way through to see how the puddings are doing – they will collapse
- ✓ I prefer to use a tray or small deep bun tins rather than one large dish. The puds seem to rise much better, and everyone I've known loves the little puffy-fluffy ones.

Fish Pie

"Fishing for compliments is never a problem with this delicious pie. I always tell my friends that there's more to fish than chips – tuck in."

Ingredients

1 lb (450 g) cod fillet, or other white fish
10 fl oz (275 ml) milk
Pinch of mixed dried herbs
1 oz (25 g) margarine
1 oz (25 g) flour
4 oz (110 g) grated Cheddar cheese
4 oz (110 g) frozen garden peas
1 lb (450 g) potatoes, boiled and mashed
2 sliced tomatoes

Method

Place the fish, with herbs, salt and pepper in a shallow pan. Pour on the milk, and poach gently for 10 minutes. Remove and flake the fish. Melt the margarine in a small pan, stir in the flour, then gradually add the liquid from the other pan. When the sauce is smooth, bring to the boil, add the peas, the flaked fish and 3 oz (75 g) of the cheese. Check for seasoning, and pour into a greased 2½ pint (1.5 l) ovenproof dish. Cover with the mashed potatoes, sprinkle with the remaining cheese and add the sliced tomatoes, overlapping them round the edge of the disk. Heat through at Gas 5, 375°F/190°C for 20 minutes.

Smoked Haddock & Mushroom Flan

"Many cooks are reluctant to embrace the magic of microwave ovens. Proper cooking, they seem to imply, takes time and a conventional oven. Well make the most of your microwave is what I say – they're marvellous! Try it with my favourite flan – smoked haddock really sets the tastebuds tingling. "

Ingredients

Serves 4-6

2 oz (50 g) lard
2 oz (50 g) margarine
8 oz (225 g) plain flour
Cold water to mix

Filling
8 oz (225 g) smoked haddock
5 fl oz (150 ml) milk
2 eggs, beaten
Pinch of salt and pepper
1 small onion, finely chopped
2 oz (50 g) mushrooms, sliced

Method 1: Microwave version

Rub the fats into the flour, and mix with cold water. Roll out, and line a 9" flan dish, pricking the base with a fork. Cook pastry on High for 3 minutes. Leave to stand. Put fish and milk into a Pyrex dish, cover with pierced cling film and cook on High for 4½ minutes. Strain off and retain liquid. Add the eggs and seasonings, and beat together. Flake the fish, removing bones and skin. Place in the bottom of the pastry case with the onion and mushrooms. Pour over the egg mixture, and cook on High for 9-10 minutes. The centre may still be moist. Let stand for 5 minutes, it should then be firm.

Method 2: Conventional Oven

Prepare the pastry and bake blind for 10 minutes at Gas 6 – 400°F, 200°C. Poach the fish in milk for 10 minutes, strain off liquid. Flake fish, and add with onion and mushrooms to flan case. Beat the eggs with the liquid, season and pour over filling. Bake in the centre of the oven, until centre is firm at Gas 6 – 400°F, 200°C.

Salmon Fish Cakes

"If you remember fishcakes as pale and boring, stop right here and get in the pink with my super salmon version – it's a fresh kind of fishcake!"

Ingredients

1 lb (450 g) potatoes
Small tin of salmon, approx 6 oz (185 g)
1 small onion, peeled and grated
1 tbsp chopped parsley
Salt and pepper
Seasoned flour
1 large egg, beaten
Browned breadcrumbs
Fat for frying

Method

Boil the potatoes, drain and mash. Mix in the onion, parsley and salt and pepper. Add the flaked salmon, using just enough of its own liquid to bind it. Divide the mixture into six or eight portions, using floured hands and flatten into round cakes. Put the seasoned flour, the egg, and breadcrumbs on three separate plates. Coat each fish cake, first in flour, then egg, and finally, breadcrumbs. Cook in hot fat, until golden each side. Can be eaten hot or cold.

Liver and Onions

"This good old Northern recipe was always a favourite with our family. On one occasion, it was my turn to cook the midday meal. But I only found two onions in the vegetable rack – not nearly enough. Then I spotted a brown paper bag on the bottom shelf. It was full of small onions, enough, thankfully, to make up the deficit. I went ahead, cooked and served the meal as usual. The following morning, I discovered my mother, trowel in hand, going through the vegetable rack. "Mildred", she said. "I bought a bag of hyacinth bulbs yesterday, and I could have sworn I put them in the vegetable rack". Oh dear! Well, no-one noticed it, and no one, thank Heaven, was any the worse, but from that day to this, I've never heard the last of it."

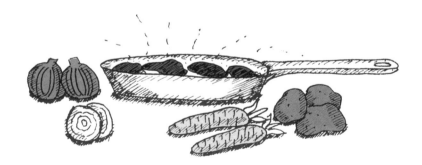

Ingredients

Serves 4

1 lb (450 g) lamb's liver
3 to 4 onions
Seasoned flour
Salt and pepper
2 oz (50 g) lard or dripping
Water or stock, about 5 fl oz (125 ml)

Method

Wash and trim the liver, coat with seasoned flour, and fry gently, until brown both sides. Remove the pan, add the onions, and fry until soft. Add the rest of the seasoned flour, stir and add the water or stock. Put the liver back into the pan, cover and cook gently for about 10 minutes.

Serve with mashed potatoes, and a green vegetable.

Liver Stroganoff

"... but Stroganoff's always made with beef!" I hear you all protesting.

Not necessarily – good cooking is characterised by inventiveness and my version of this classic dish is a very tasty and economical alternative.

For the health-conscious cook, plain yoghurt is a good substitute for the cream – although, in my house I must admit that the cream is always a favourite!"

Ingredients

1 lb (450 g) lamb's liver and 2 rashers streaky bacon,
    chopped
1 onion, peeled and chopped
4 oz (110 g) mushrooms, sliced
2 tbsp seasoned flour
3 oz (75 g) margarine
10 fl oz (275 ml) chicken stock
5 fl oz (150 ml) carton soured cream or plain yoghurt.

Method

Cut the liver into strips, and toss in the seasoned flour. Fry in half the margarine until lightly browned. Remove from the pan, and keep warm. Fry the onion, bacon and mushrooms in the remaining fat.

Stir in the remaining seasoned flour, gradually blend in the stock, bring gently to the boil. Return the liver to the pan and cook for 1 – 2 minutes. Take the pan off the heat, check the seasoning, add the cream or yoghurt and reheat.

Serve with plain boiled rice, or creamed potatoes, as preferred.

Baked Meat Loaf

"Meat loaf makes sense in a microwave. You'll have a delicious meal in less than half an hour – just enough time for a pre-dinner sherry!"

Ingredients

1 lb (450 g) minced beef
1 onion, peeled and chopped
1 egg, beaten
2 oz (50 g) white breadcrumbs
1 oz (25 g) margarine
2 tsp dried peppers

Method

Pour hot water over the peppers and leave for 20 minutes. Mix the meat, onion and breadcrumbs. Drain and add the peppers. Add the margarine, egg and season with salt and pepper. Spoon into a greased 1 lb loaf tin, and place in a roasting tin, with a little water round it. Cook at Gas 4 – 350°F, 180°C for 1½ hours. Leave to cool in the tin before turning out.

May be eaten hot or cold, and will freeze well wrapped in foil.

Microwave Version:

It may also be cooked in the microwave. Follow the instructions, but use a Pyrex or Microwave safe container. It should take about 18 minutes in a 650 Watt microwave.

Pork with Pepper and Tomato Sauce

"A great way to cheer up your chops – simply delicious."

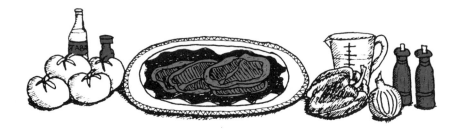

Ingredients

Serves 4

4 large lean pork chops
1 onion, peeled and chopped
1 green pepper, deseeded and chopped
1 tbsp Tabasco (or other hot sauce)
5 fl oz (150 ml) stock
Pinch of basil or mixed dried herbs
Salt and pepper
1lb (450 g) tomatoes, skinned and chopped, or a large
    can of chopped tomatoes.

Method

Fry or grill the chops, drain and set aside. Fry the onion in the fat left over from cooking chops or a little fresh fat, if you grilled them. Add all the remaining ingredients and bring to the boil, then simmer for 5 minutes. Put the chops back in the pan and simmer for a further 5 minutes.

Chicken Casserole

"Chicken's the choice as my family's favourite casserole, so chuck 'em a treat with this wonderful winter warmer!"

Ingredients

Serves 4

4 chicken portions
2 oz (50 g) plain flour seasoned with salt and pepper
2 oz (50 g) butter or margarine
1 onion, peeled and chopped
4 tomatoes, peeled and chopped
2 red peppers, deseeded and sliced (or 2 tbsp
    reconstituted dried peppers).
15 fl oz (425 ml) chicken stock

Method

Preheat the oven to moderate, Gas 4 – 180°C, 350°F. Coat the chicken pieces in the seasoned flour. Fry on all sides in the fat until golden. Place in a greased casserole. Fry the onion in the remaining fat. Add the stock, tomatoes and onion to the casserole. Cover and cook in the centre of the oven for 1 hour. Add the sliced peppers and cook for 15 minutes more.

Microwave method

This casserole may be cooked in the microwave. Add all the ingredients, including the chicken portions, but not the flour or butter. Cook on high for 18 minutes, taking out and stirring half-way through. Take out a little of the stock, mix with the flour and cook for 2 minutes longer. This works well with a 650 Watt oven. Check your own microwave settings.

Chicken Pancakes

"It's no toss-up between sweet and savoury when chicken's the choice for pancakes – go on, fry up a feast!"

Ingredients

Makes 6 Pancakes:

Batter
    4 oz (110 g) flour
    1 egg
    10 fl oz (275 ml) milk
    Pinch of salt

Method
Make the batter, exactly as for Yorkshire Pudding. (see recipe on page 34) allow to stand for 1 hour, then make the pancakes and keep warm.

Filling
    1lb (450 g) cooked diced chicken
    4 oz (110 g) chopped mushrooms
    Juice of half a lemon
    2 tbsp butter or margarine
    2 tbsp cream
    1 tsp chopped chives and onion
    1 tbsp Parmesan cheese, grated
    $\frac{1}{2}$ tbsp flour, with a pinch of cayenne pepper
    Salt and pepper

Method

Melt $1\frac{1}{2}$ tablespoons of the butter over a low heat. Stir in lemon juice and chicken and cook gently for 5 minutes. Add mushrooms, chives and a little salt and pepper and cook gently for a further 5 minutes. Cream remaining butter with the flour, add cream, add to the pan and cook for 2-3 more minutes.

Divide the mixture between the pancakes, roll up, and sprinkle with the Parmesan cheese.

The Great Sausage Story

Sausages may be commonplace today but during the war they were a rare thing. Hardly ever in stock and, when they were, rationing allowed only one sausage per person.

Just after the war, when I was a clippie on the trams, we were trundling through Longsight one day and there, in a butcher's window, was a plate piled so high with sausages, I could hardly believe my eyes! My tram pulled up at some traffic lights and I could scarcely contain myself. Did I have time to run in whilst the lights were on red – and would the butcher let me have more than one sausage? The lights were still red and my mind was made up.

I dashed into the shop, made my request and to my delight the butcher said 'One or two? You can have a pound!' I hurriedly paid and dashed out again clutching my prize – only to see the sad sight of my tram disappearing out of view. As I started to chase it, shouting in vain for the driver to stop, I noticed people laughing at me. My parcel had come undone and I was running along with two strings of sausages flying behind me in the wind!

So desperate was I to retrieve my tram, I stopped an oncoming lorry, hopped on and said 'follow that tram.' He did (nice chap) and, after two miles of chasing, I was able to rejoin my tram.

Whew! So you can see why sausages will never be commonplace to me.

Enjoy!"

Sausage Risotto

Ingredients

Serves 4

8 oz (225 g) sausages
4 oz (110 g) long-grain rice
8 oz (225 g) tomatoes, skinned and sliced
1 onion, peeled and sliced
2 sticks of celery, sliced
4 oz (110 g) frozen peas
½ red or green pepper, diced
2 oz (50 g) butter
Pinch of mixed herbs
Salt and Pepper

Method

Cook the rice in boiling salted water for 20 minutes. After 10 minutes add the peas to the pan. Grill the sausage, cool slightly and slice. Melt the butter in a frying pan, and cook the onion, celery and pepper until soft. Add the tomatoes, cook for 2-3 minutes more, then add rice and herbs, and lastly, slice sausage and heat through.

Note: Instead of sausage, fish fingers, grilled and cut into pieces may be added. (Often popular with children, and a good way to include vegetables).

Sausage & Capers

"For a perfectly piquant pan-full, pop in the capers and pep up those pork sausages for a right proper treat!"

Ingredients

Serves 4

1 lb (450 g) pork sausages
8 oz (225 g) onions, peeled and thinly sliced
4 large tomatoes, skinned and sliced
1 rounded tbsp capers
10 fl oz (275 ml) of chicken stock
Salt and black pepper

Method

Preheat the oven to Gas 5, 190°C or 375°F.

Arrange the onions in the base of a shallow casserole. Cover with sliced tomatoes. Sprinkle capers over the top, season and add stock. Lay the sausage on top, cover with lid or foil and cook in the centre of the oven for 30-40 minutes. Check that the onions are tender. Remove lid or foil, and cook for further 10 minutes or until sausages are brown.

Serve with mashed potatoes.

Hashed Beef or Lamb

"When the weekend roast's just a memory,
and the leftovers are looking sad,
make an old-fashioned hash of it,
(but don't make a mess of it),
for the best meal you've ever had."

Ingredients

Serves 4

1 lb (450 g) cooked beef or lamb, cut in slices
8 oz (225 g) dried beans, haricot, butter, or red kidney,
   as available
2 large onions, peeled and quartered
4 oz (110 g) mushrooms, wiped and sliced
12 oz (350 g) tomatoes, skinned and quartered
1 pint (570 ml) of brown stock
2 oz (50 g) butter or margarine
1 oz (25 g) flour
1 tsp mixed dried herbs
1 tsp sugar
salt and pepper

Method

Cover the beans with cold water and soak overnight. Next day drain, cover with fresh water and boil gently until tender, about 35 minutes. Melt ½ the butter and fry the onions gently until soft. Lift out with a slotted spoon and place in a shallow, greased, casserole dish. In the same butter, fry the mushrooms, lightly and place on top of the onions. Lay the slices of meat on top and season. Melt the remaining butter in the same pan, stir in the flour and add the stock gradually, stirring to make a thin, smooth sauce. Drain the cooked beans and layer over the meat. Sprinkle with the herbs and pour in the stock, lay the tomatoes on top, season and sprinkle with the sugar. Cook the casserole, uncovered in the centre of the oven for 30-40 minutes at Gas 4 – 180°C, 350°F. Serve with a green salad and crusty bread or plain boiled rice.

Note: Tinned beans may be used. Drain, rinse and add to the casserole at the same stage as the boiled dried beans.

Cheesy Lamb Crumble

"Liven up leftover lamb with a creative crumble that's just the job – a crunchy cheesy treat!"

Ingredients

¾ lb (340 g) cold cooked lamb
1 medium onion
2 stock cubes (lamb or beef)
10 fl oz (275 ml) hot water
1 dessert spoon tomato puree
4½ oz (125 g) flour
2 oz (50 g) butter
2 oz (50 g) grated cheese
1 level tsp mixed herbs
Salt & pepper

Method

Mince the lamb and onion together. Dissolve the stock cubes in the hot water and add the tomato puree. Add to the minced meat. Sprinkle with salt and pepper or add ½oz (25 g) of flour. Mix well and turn into a greased baking dish. Rub the butter into the flour until it looks like breadcrumbs, stir in the cheese and herbs, salt and pepper. Spoon over the meat.

Bake at Gas 6 – 200°C, 400°F for 40-45 minutes. Serve with grilled mushrooms and any green vegetable.

Bacon Ribs and Vegetables, All-in-One

"Here's a real rib-tickler; it's tasty and tempting, and easy to prepare."

Ingredients

Serves 4

Two sheets of bacon ribs, weighing about (lb 450 g) each
1½-2lbs (675-900 g) spring cabbage
4 medium onions, peeled and quartered
4 carrots, cleaned and cut in chunks
4 medium potatoes, peeled and quartered
Water
A very little salt and pepper

Method

Break each sheet of ribs into 2 pieces, or as will go into a large pan, cover with water, bring to the boil and boil gently for 30 minutes. If using a pressure cooker, cook for 20 minutes. Take out the ribs and throw away the water. This removes excess salt. Put the potatoes, onions and carrots into the pan, cover with water, bring to the boil and cook for 15 minutes. Wash and shred the spring cabbage, put on top of the other vegetables, lay the bacon ribs on top, cover or partially cover and cook for 10 minutes. Seasoning is usually not necessary, as the ribs flavour the other vegetables. If used – use sparingly. Serve straight from the pan.

Note: This dish is especially good for the health conscious or those on low-fat diets, as no fat is used in the cooking.

Lobby or Lobscouse

"Lobscouse is an old Liverpool favourite. Seafarers made it with salt beef, but everyone enjoys it nowadays."

Ingredients

Serves 4

1lb (450 g) stewing steak
2lbs (900 g) potatoes, peeled and halved
1 onion, skinned and quartered
1 carrot, scraped and sliced
6 oz (150 g) dried peas, soaked overnight
1½ pints (850 ml) of stock
¼ tsp chopped mint
¼ tsp chopped or dried thyme
2 oz (50 g) butter or dripping
Salt and pepper

Method

Trim excess fat from the meat and cut into cubes. Melt the fat in bottom of a deep casserole. Put in the potatoes, carrot and onion and lay the cubed beef on top. Drain the peas and add to the dish. Add the thyme, mint, a little salt and pepper. Pour on the warmed stock, adding a little water if not sufficient to just cover the peas. Cover with the lid, or foil and cook for 3 – 4 hours, Gas 2 – 150°C, 300°F. Serve straight from the pot.

Note: This dish may be made just as easily in a slow cooker. This dish was originally made with salt beef but, as you don't seem to see it nowadays, I use stewing steak instead.

Frying Pan Supper

"For an all-in-one that's one-for-all, fetch out the frying pan and stir up a traditional treat!"

Ingredients

Serves 2

 1 lb (450 g) potatoes, cooked and cubed
 4 oz (110 g) mushrooms, wiped and sliced
 4 oz (110 g) frozen peas
 7 oz (175 g) can chopped ham or pork, cut into $\frac{1}{2}$" cubes
 2 level tsp ready-mixed mustard
 2 tbsp mayonnaise or salad cream
 1 hard-boiled egg, chopped
 1 oz (25 g) butter or margarine
 Few spring onions, trimmed and chopped
 Salt and pepper

Method

In a large frying-pan, heat the butter or margarine, add the mushrooms and peas, and cook gently for 5 minutes. Stir in the mustard and mayonnaise, then add the ham, potatoes and finally the spring onions. Cook over a moderate heat for about 8 minutes, turning the mixture constantly to heat through. Just before serving, stir in the egg.

Note: This recipe is especially nice if small new potatoes are used, cut in half.

Mince & Potato Bake

"Make more with mince, I always say, for a satisfying dish on a cold winter's day."

Ingredients

Serves 4

1 tbsp oil and $\frac{1}{2}$ oz (15 g) butter
$1\frac{1}{2}$ lb (675 g) minced beef
2 medium onions
14 oz (350 g) tin chopped tomatoes or 6 fresh, skinned
  and chopped
3 medium potatoes
1 tsp dried mixed herbs
Salt and pepper

Method

Heat the oil and butter together in a large frying-pan. Fry the onions until soft. Add the mince and fry, stirring until it has browned all over. Add the tomatoes, with their juice. (If fresh use tomato puree and water). Stir in the herbs, bring to the boil, then turn down the heat and simmer for 20 minutes. Meanwhile, peel and slice the potatoes, thinly. Turn the mince into a greased ovenproof dish, arrange the potato slices on top, overlapping, brush with a little more oil, and bake for 30-40 minutes until the potatoes are golden brown, Gas 6 – 200°C, 400°F.

Note: Minced lamb or pork can be used instead of beef.

The Vegetarian Vote

There's an old Indian proverb which says: "A meal without flesh is like feeding on grass."

A lot of people make the mistake of

thinking that vegetarian food is boring and tasteless. Not so in my book (if you'll pardon the pun . . .) – I've many friends now who don't eat meat and the possibilities are endless. Try a few of my suggestions and you'll soon see how wrong that old proverb was!"

Broccoli Flan

"Bring out the broccoli for a flan-tastic treat – much better than a quick quiche any day."

Ingredients

Serves 4

6 oz (150 g) shortcrust pastry
5 oz (125 g) broccoli, cut into small florets
1 medium onion, peeled and chopped
2 eggs, size 3, beaten
4 oz (110 g) Cheddar cheese, grated
Salt and black pepper
10 fl oz (275 ml) milk

Method

Line an 8" flan ring or dish with the pastry. Cover the onion in boiling water, boil for 2 minutes, add the broccoli and boil for 2 minutes more. Drain well. Place in the pastry case. Beat the eggs and milk together, season well and pour over the broccoli and onion. Sprinkle the cheese over the top and bake for about 40-45 minutes, until golden brown and set. Gas 5 – 190°C, 375°F.

Cheesy Bake

"As a side-dish for supper,
or the main dish for lunch,
choose a cheesy bake –
for the family to munch."

Ingredients

Serves 4

1 lb (450 g) potatoes
2 medium onions
1 tsp vegetable extract
1 tsp dry mustard
10 – 12 oz (250 – 350 g) cottage cheese
1 tsp mixed dried herbs
4 oz (110 g) hard cheese, grated
2 or 3 tomatoes, sliced
Parsley for garnish

Method

Cut the potatoes and onions into thick slices and cook for about 15 minutes in boiling, salted water. Mix the extract and mustard with 1 tbsp of the hot water. Drain cooked potatoes and onions and mash together with the cottage cheese, salt and pepper, herbs and the mustard mixture. (A little butter may be added at this stage, if liked). Put into a greased ovenproof dish, sprinkle with grated cheese and arranged sliced tomato on top. Bake for 10-15 minutes at Gas 7 – 220°C, 425°F. Garnish with parsley and serve with a green vegetable.

Spanish Omelette

"Even the smallest Spanish restaurant serves up their own version of this famous dish. It's a satisfying lunch-time snack or a perfect main meal."

Ingredients

Serves 4

6 eggs
2 large potatoes
1 large onion, peeled and chopped
Half red pepper, deseeded and sliced
Half green pepper, deseeded and sliced
Salt and black pepper
Butter or oil for frying

Method

Boil the potatoes, and dice. Melt a little butter or oil in a large frying-pan and fry the chopped onions until soft. Do not brown. Beat the eggs and season with salt and pepper. Add the peppers to the pan and fry for 2 minutes. Pour in the egg mixture and cook gently, lifting at the sides to let the mixture run beneath. When almost cooked, the top will still be runny. Place the frying-pan under a fairly hot grill, until the top sets. Serve with a green salad, and brown bread and butter.

Lentil Pie

"There's plenty of protein in this lovely pie,
pulsating with goodness –
you should give it a try."

Ingredients

Serves 4

4 oz (110 g) lentils
1 onion, peeled and finely chopped
3 small carrots, peeled and diced
3 small courgettes, trimmed and diced
3 sticks celery, thinly sliced
1 lb (450 g) potatoes, peeled and diced
1 tbsp tomato puree
2 tbsp oil
1 vegetable stock cube
10 fl oz (275 ml) water
1 oz (25 g) butter or margarine
1 tbsp milk
4 oz (110 g) cheese, grated

Method

Set the oven to Gas 7 – 220°C, 425°F. Heat 1 tbsp oil in a saucepan, cook the onion until soft, (5 minutes). Add the lentils, water and stock cube, stir and bring to the boil. Reduce the heat and simmer for 20 minutes, until the lentils are softened, and have absorbed most of the liquid. In another saucepan, heat the remaining oil and add the carrots, courgettes and celery. Cover and cook for 10-15 minutes, until softened. Cook the potatoes in boiling salted water, then drain well. Stir the tomato puree into the lentil mixture and mix in the vegetables. Season. Mash the potatoes, beat in the butter or margarine, milk and three-quarters of the cheese. Put the lentil mixture, into a greased dish, top with the mashed potato and sprinkle with the rest of the cheese. Bake in the centre of the oven 20-25 minutes, or until golden-brown. Serve with a green vegetable or salad.

Curried Cauliflower and Eggs

"Curry family favour with a spicy flavour and change your cauli forever – a hot and tasty treat!"

Ingredients

Serves 4

1 medium cauliflower
3 oz (75 g) butter or margarine
2 tomatoes, peeled and chopped
2 sticks of celery, chopped
1 large onion, peeled and chopped
5 fl oz (150 ml) vegetable stock
1 dessertspoon curry powder
1 tbsp chutney
2 hard-boiled eggs, chopped

Method

Wash the cauliflower, break into small sprigs, blanch in boiling, salted water for 2 minutes, then drain well. Melt the butter in a large frying-pan. Toss the cauliflower in this for a few minutes, then add the tomatoes, celery and onion. Mix together the rest of the ingredients, except the eggs, and add to the pan. Cover and simmer for 10 minutes, then sprinkle with the chopped egg. Serve with plain, boiled rice, or naan bread.

A Load of Tripe

"A gentleman who reviewed my last book complained of the absence of tripe recipes. He musn't have looked properly, because the classic one was there. I was, however, inspired to take up his challenge to include some tripe dishes even he couldn't miss. Go on, try some tripe!"

Fried Tripe

Ingredients

1 lb (450 g) Honeycomb Tripe
2 tbsp salad oil
1 tbsp chopped onion
1 tbsp lemon juice
1 egg
A little flour
Breadcrumbs
Salt and pepper

Method

Cut the tripe into bite-size pieces. On a plate, mix the oil, onion, lemon-juice and seasoning. Marinate the tripe in this mixture for 30 minutes. Drain the pieces on paper, coat lightly with flour and dip in the beaten egg, to which has been added a little water and salt and pepper. Coat with breadcrumbs and fry in hot fat until browned all over. Drain and serve hot, garnished with parsley.

Tripe Fritters

Ingredients

1 lb (450 g) Honeycomb Tripe
1 dessertspoon chopped parsley
Pepper and salt, lemon Juice
Fat for frying

For the batter:
4 oz (110 g) flour
1 egg
Pinch of salt
Small teacup of tepid milk

Method

Cut the tripe into 2" square and dry well. Sprinkle with the parsley, lemon juice and seasonings. Prepare the batter one hour before and beat well before using. Dip each piece of tripe into the batter and fry until golden-brown. Drain and serve hot, garnished with parsley. (Serve with creamed potatoes, and baked beans in tomato sauce for a very nourishing meal).

Tripe Salad

Method

Cut a pound of Tripe into shreds, and pour on some salad dressing. Place in the centre of a serving dish, surrounded by lettuce or garnished with tomato slices and quartered hard boiled eggs.

Quick Salad Dressing

Method

Mix 2 tbsp oil with 1 tbsp vinegar. Add a pinch of salt, shake of pepper and small amount of ready-mixed mustard. A pinch of sugar may also be added.

Savoury Tripe

Ingredients

1½ lb (675 g) of tripe
½ lb (225 g) tomatoes
¼ lb (110 g) mushrooms
1½ oz (40 g) lard or dripping
1 tbsp flour
1 pint (570 ml) of stock (vegetable) or water
Salt and pepper
2 tbsp breadcrumbs
A little grated cheese

Method

Wipe the tomatoes and cut in thick slices. Peel and slice the mushrooms. Melt the fat in a saucepan, and fry tomatoes and mushrooms for a few minutes, then lift out and onto a plate. Add the flour to the fat and brown it slightly. Pour in the stock and stir until boiling, season to taste. Cut the tripe into bite-size pieces and lay them in a greased pie-dish. Cover with the tomatoes and mushrooms. Pour on the brown sauce. Sprinkle with the breadcrumbs and cheese. Cook at Gas 4 – 180°C, 350°F for 30 minutes.

Tripe as a Light Supper Dish

Ingredients

2 lbs (900 g) Honeycomb Tripe
2 tsp Bovril
3 ripe tomatoes, skinned and sliced
3 oz (75 g) grated cheese
1 lb (450 g) mashed potatoes
1 tsp chopped parsley

Method

Cut the tripe into pieces, cover with cold water, bring to boil and simmer for 5 minutes. Add the Bovril, season with salt and pepper and stir to mix thoroughly. Put into an oven-proof dish: Cover with the tomatoes, sprinkle on the cheese, and top with mashed potatoes. Cook at Gas 4 – 180°C, 350°F until the top is golden-brown. Sprinkle with parsley and serve hot.

Desserts

"Let them eat cake" said Marie Antoinette

– she wouldn't have said it if she'd tasted my early attempts, nor my puddings, as I had that typically youthful characteristic of the wandering mind.

One time I remember well was when I tried to combine cooking and piano practice. All was going well and once the pudding was done and boiling away I (being the industrious type) started practising at the piano. So absorbed was I that the pudding boiled dry! It was forever after known in my family as the Sonata Pudding. The moral of this story? Keep your mind on your cooking and your eye on the pudding!

The Great Courgette Crisis

"If you're at all surprised to see courgettes in the dessert section, let me explain how I fell upon this unusual recipe. When my green-fingered husband first discovered courgettes he decided we shouldn't buy them, we should grow our own. "Lovely," I said – little did I realise that he would grow enough to feed the whole population of Stockport for a year! Day after day, more and more courgettes appeared in my kitchen. I baked them, fried them, boiled them, and even cut them into chips. But still they kept coming, and bigger and bigger they grew too. I baked and stuffed them and began to detest them, and even had nightmares of being chased by rampant, giant courgettes!"

My husband finally listened to my pleas when I threatened to divorce him unless the courgettes stopped. My Courgette Tart was an inspired way of using the surplus supplies. I hope you like it.

Courgette Tart

Ingredients

Serves 6

8 oz (225 g) shortcrust pastry
2 teacups of peeled and grated courgettes
2 eggs, beaten
4 oz (110 g) light brown sugar
One level tsp cinnamon
A few drops of vanilla essence
A little milk

Method

Grease an 8" pie plate, and line with pastry. Mix together the beaten eggs and sugar, stir in the courgettes, add a little milk if the mix seems a bit stiff, and finally add the cinnamon and vanilla. Put into the pastry case; Roll out the remaining pastry and cut into strips to make a lattice top. Bake at Gas 6 – 200°C, 400°F – for 10 minutes, then turn down the heat and bake for about 20 minutes more, or until pastry is golden. Serve with cream.

Lemon Pudding

"This lemony treat will make your taste buds tingle. Maybe it's because it's so light that it disappears so quickly!"

Ingredients

2½ oz (75 g) self-raising flour
7 oz (175 g) caster sugar
2 oz (50 g) margarine
2 eggs
1 lemon
5 tbsp milk
4 tbsp water

Method

Cream the fat and sugar. Separate the yolks from the whites, and beat the yolks into the creamed mixture. Fold in half of the sieved flour, and the grated rind and juice of the lemon. Fold in the remaining flour, the milk and water and stiffly beaten egg whites. Pour the mixture into a greased pie dish and cook at Gas 3, 325°F, 160°C for about 1 hour. Serve with cream.

Note: You may think the liquid content is high, but during the cooking, the light sponge rises to the top and the liquids form a lemony sauce.

Rhubarb & Orange Crumble

"Rhubarb, rhubarb, rhubarb..." It has a poor reputation, don't you think? Unnecessarily so in my opinion – this dish changed the view of a friend of mine, previously scornful of this humble fruit. It'll change your mind too!

Ingredients

Serves 4

For the crumble

4 oz (110 g) self-raising flour and pinch of salt
2 oz (50 g) margarine
2 oz (50 g) sugar

For the filling

About 10 oz (300 g) rhubarb cut into half-inch pieces
1 large orange – rind and juice
2 oz (50 g) sultanas
Sugar to sweeten. Sweeten well, rhubarb is tart!

Method

Rub the margarine into the flour until it looks like bread-crumbs, then add the sugar and mix well. Put the rhubarb into a pan. Mix the orange juice with just enough water to cover the fruit. Bring gently to the boil, turn down and simmer for 5 minutes. Remove from the heat, sweeten to taste, allow it to cool a little, then add the orange rind and sultanas. Put into a greased pie-dish. Sprinkle the crumble mixture over the top. Bake for about 30 minutes or until golden brown at Gas 5 – 190°C, 375°F. Serve with cream or custard.

Microwave Coffee Pudding – in an Instant!

"You've always got time for this pudding . . . after all, microwaves do make melting moments!"

Ingredients

Serves 4-6

- 4 oz (110 g) margarine
- 4 oz (110 g) caster sugar
- 2 eggs, beaten
- 3 oz (75 g) self-raising flour, with a pinch of bicarbonate of soda
- 1 oz (25 g) cocoa
- 10 fl oz (275 ml) strong black coffee – sweetened. (Add rum if liked)
- 10 fl oz (275 ml) double cream, or packet of 'instant' dessert topping.
- 2 oz (50 g) flaked almonds, toasted.

Method

Cream the margarine and sugar together. Add the eggs and the flour and cocoa alternately, mixing well. Put into a lightly greased 1½ pint (850 ml) pudding basin, and cover loosely with cling film. Cook on high for 4-5 minutes (650 watts). Test by seeing if sponge comes away from side of basin. Leave in the basin, but allow to cool. Make the coffee, sweeten to taste and pour over the pudding, using a fork to ease away from sides and let the liquid run down. Put in a cold place and leave for at least 2 hours. Turn out and coat the top and sides with cream (or topping) and nuts. (For an attractive finish, toast the nuts on a plate in the microwave for 2-3 minutes, turning over 2 or 3 times.)

Custard Tart

"Custard tarts are the stuff of slap-stick comedy, but this one's no joke – it's top of the bill in our house."

Ingredients

4 oz (110 g) shortcrust pastry
2 eggs
10 fl oz (275 ml) milk
2 tbsp sugar
Ground nutmeg

Method

Make the pastry, with 4 oz (110 g) flour and 2 oz (50 g) lard and margarine. Grease a 7" flan tin. Line with pastry and bake blind for 10 minutes in an oven preheated to Gas 5 – 190°C, 375°F. Reduce heat to Gas 4 – 180°C, 350°F. Prepare the filling by heating the milk and sugar together. Whisk the eggs, pour on the milk and allow to cool. Pour carefully into the prepared pastry case and sprinkle with nutmeg. Bake for about 20 minutes or until set.

Apple Batter Pudding

"Old-fashioned gardens nearly always had apple trees, so we looked for ways to use our cooking apples. Here's one of my all-time favourites."

Ingredients

Serves 4-6

Set the oven to hot: Gas 6, 200°C, 400°F.
2 oz (50 g) self-raising flour
2 large eggs
5 fl oz (150 ml) milk and water mixed
$1\frac{1}{4}$ lb (550 g) cooking apples
3 oz (75 g) light brown sugar
2 level tbsp chopped mixed nuts
$\frac{1}{2}$ level tsp cinnamon
2 pint oven-proof dish, well oiled.

Method

Sift the flour into a bowl. Drop in the eggs. Stir flour from the sides of the bowl, beating until smooth and gradually add the milk and water. Peel, quarter, and core the apples, then slice them into a bowl. Stir in 2 oz (50 g) of the sugar, the nuts, and cinnamon. Transfer to the oven-proof dish. Pour over the batter. Sprinkle on the remaining sugar. Bake above centre of the oven until slightly risen and golden brown. Serve with single cream.

Orange Marmalade Tart

"Marmalade's not just for spreading on toast, you know. This tasty tart is so easy to make – and will they ever guess what you've used?"

Ingredients

6 oz (150 g) shortcrust pastry i.e. 6 oz flour, 3 oz fat
6 tbsp orange marmalade, preferably thick cut
2 small eggs, beaten
1 tbsp whisky
Double cream
Grated rind of an orange
A little icing sugar

Method

Grease an 8" shallow pie plate, and line with pastry. Mix the beaten eggs into the marmalade, and add the whisky. Pour into the pastry case and use the remaining pastry, cut into strips to make a lattice topping. Bake at Gas 6 – 200°C, or 400°F until pastry is golden brown. Sieve a little icing sugar into the cream and mix in the orange rind. Serve together

Puzzle Pudding

"This pudding is so-named because it is puzzling that anything so simple can taste so good. Try it and see!"

Ingredients

4 oz (110 g) self-raising flour and a pinch of salt
2 oz (50 g) suet
2 oz (50 g) golden syrup
Milk to mix

Method: conventional

Mix all the ingredients together, adding just enough milk to make a soft dough. Put into a large greased pudding basin, cover loosely with a cloth or cling film. Steam for 1½ hours.

Microwave method

This pudding can also be made in the microwave, but check your own microwave manual for directions for sponge pudding. Allow a little less time for this pudding, as the syrup content makes for faster cooking. I allow about 4 minutes at 650 watts.

Serve with custard, or marmalade sauce, or both.

For marmalade sauce, heat 2 heaped tbsp of marmalade with 1 tbsp water, a squeeze of lemon and a little sugar in the microwave.

Christmas Pudding (Microwave)

"There's nothing like home-made Christmas Puddings, but they take so long to bake! Microwaves to the rescue – in less than an hour you'll have a perfect pud."

Ingredients

This recipe makes one 2lb (900g) or two 1lb (450g) puddings.

4 oz (110 g) margarine
2 tbsp black treacle
8 oz (225 g) currants
5 oz (125 g) raisins
5 oz (125 g) sultanas
[In place of the currants, raisins and sultanas, you can use 1lb 2 oz (500 g) mixed dried fruit]
8 oz (225 g) soft dark brown sugar
1 tsp ground ginger
2 tsp mixed spice
6 oz (150 g) brown breadcrumbs
3 oz (75 g) plain flour
3 eggs (size 3) beaten
rind and juice of an orange
5 fl oz (150 ml) stout

Method

Melt the margarine and treacle over a low heat. Add all remaining ingredients and mix thoroughly. Put into a large bowl and cook in the microwave, uncovered, on High for 6 minutes, stirring every minute until mixture starts to bubble on the surface. Lightly grease pudding basins (2½pt size for a large pudding or two 1½pt ones for smaller puddings). Smooth the surface and cover loosely with greased greaseproof paper. Cook on 'defrost': 23-25 minutes for large; 12-13 minutes each for smaller puddings. They will be ready when firm to the touch. Leave to stand for 15 minutes before turning out. Wash the bowls before replacing puddings. Store for up to 2 months. Reheat on Defrost: 8-10 minutes for large; 5-7 minutes for small.

Pineapple and Apple Fritters

"**Warning:** do not attempt to make these puddings unless you're prepared to accept the calorific consequences! Yes, I'll admit it – the calorie content in these two puds is higher than this year's pollen count! But boy are they delicious! Go on, treat yourself."

Pineapple Fritters

Ingredients

Serves 4
- 1 large can pineapple rings (8) 1lb 14 oz (900 g)
- 4 oz (110 g) self-raising flour
- 2 level tsp baking powder
- 5 fl oz (150 ml) milk
- Deep fat for frying

Method

Sieve the flour and baking powder together. Add milk gradually, beating to make a smooth, thick batter. Drain and dry the pineapple rings. Dip them in the batter, coating completely. Fry in hot, deep fat until golden brown. Serve hot, sprinkled with caster sugar.

Apple Fritters

Method

Peel and core apples, cut into rings and follow the above recipe. If the apples are tart sprinkle with sugar before dipping into the batter.

Sticky Toffee Pudding

"... as seen on the menus of all the best restaurants. It's funny how fashions change, but this is the stickiest, toffeeist pudding imagineable!"

Ingredients

6 oz (150 g) dates
10 fl oz (275 ml) water
1 level tsp bicarbonate of soda
2 oz (50 g) butter, preferably unsalted
6 oz (100 g) caster sugar
2 eggs, beaten
6 oz (100 g) self-raising flour
10 fl oz (275 ml) of double cream
2 oz (50 g) light brown sugar, or demerara sugar
2 tsp golden syrup

Method

Put the dates and water into a saucepan, bring to the boil and boil for 5 minutes. Remove from the heat, add the bicarb and leave to cool. Cream the butter and caster sugar together, add the eggs, then the flour and finally the date mixture, drained. Bake in an oven-proof dish at Gas 4 – 180°C, 350°F for 30-35 minutes, until firm. Put the cream, sugar and syrup into a saucepan, bring to the boil and boil, stirring until the mixture becomes golden-brown and thickens. When the cake is done, some of the toffee sauce may be poured over the top and grilled for a couple of minutes. (Optional: Serve with the remaining sauce poured over!)

Banoffee Pie

"Here's another popular toffee pud –
bananas add such a smooth touch to
this tempting favourite."

Ingredients – makes an 8" pie

5 oz (125 g) plain flour
8 oz (225 g) butter
2 oz (50 g) caster sugar
14 oz (450 g) can condensed milk
4 oz (110 g) light brown sugar
2 small bananas
2 tbsp golden syrup

To Decorate

1 banana
A little lemon juice
Whipped cream
1 tsp grated plain chocolate

Method

Rub 4 oz (110 g) of the butter into the flour, add the caster sugar, and continue rubbing in until like breadcrumbs. Squeeze the mixture into a dough with your hands (like making a shortcake). Roll into a ball, put into the bottom of a greased, loose-bottomed 8" flan tin, and spread it out to fill. Bake at Gas 3 – 160°C, 325°F – for 25 minutes, or until light brown. Leave to cool. Put the condensed milk, the remaining butter, brown sugar and syrup into a pan. Bring to the boil and boil for 7 minutes, stirring all the time to prevent burning. Slice the two bananas and line the pastry case. Pour over the toffee filling and leave to cool completely. Decorate with the whipped cream, the remaining banana (dipped in lemon juice to prevent browning) and the grated chocolate.

Cakes and Bakes

Ginger Cake

"This recipe was given to me by an elderly lady, for whom I have the greatest respect, not only for her culinary expertise, but for her unfailing kindness and friendship. Like the donor, it is a family favourite."

Ingredients

8 oz (225 g) self-raising flour
4 oz (110 g) margarine
4 oz (110 g) caster sugar
2 tbsp golden syrup
2 eggs, beaten
2 tsp ginger
½ teacup of warm milk
½ tsp bicarbonate of soda

Method

Rub the margarine into the flour. Add the sugar and ginger. Dissolve the bicarbonate of soda in the milk and add with the beaten eggs and syrup to the mixture and stir well. Pour into a greased 7" cake tin. Bake at Gas 3 – 160°C 325°F – for 1 hour 10 minutes – 1 hour 15 minutes.

Chocolate Delight

"There's something mysterious about Chocolate Delight . . . make it . . . and it disappears – just like that!"

Ingredients

1 packet of rich tea or Marie biscuits
8 oz (225 g) butter or margarine
2 rounded dessertspoons brown sugar
3 dessertspoons drinking chocolate or cocoa
3 tbsp golden syrup
4 oz (110 g) sultanas

For the topping:
12 oz (350 g) plain cooking chocolate

Method

Break the biscuits into small pieces – not crumbs. Over a low heat, melt together the margarine, sugar, drinking chocolate, syrup and sultanas. Stir in the broken biscuits, mixing thoroughly. Grease a shallow tray and spoon in the mixture, pressing well down. Melt the cooking chocolate in a basin over a pan of hot water and spread evenly over the mix. Leave in a cold place to set. Cut into fingers and store in an air-tight container.

Sooty Cake

"When my granddaughter was small, this was her favourite cake – and I was in big trouble if I hadn't made one for her visits. What she won't admit now is – it's still her favourite. But don't tell anyone..."

Ingredients

8 oz (225 g) plain flour
1 level tsp bicarbonate of soda
4 oz (110 g) butter or margarine
8 oz (225 g) granulated sugar
2 large eggs, beaten
1 oz (25 g) cocoa
1 can of stout (9 fl oz – 250 ml)

Method

Grease and line an 8" tin, preferably a clip tin. If using a clip tin, line the base only.

Set the oven to Gas 4, 180°C, 350°F. Cream the fat with the sugar until soft. Add the eggs, a little at a time, beating well after each addition. Blend the cocoa with a little of the stout in a basin, then stir in the rest of the stout. Sift the flour and bicarb together and stir into the creamed mixture, alternatively with the stout liquid. Don't worry if the mixture appears to curdle at first, this will disappear as more flour is added. Pour into the prepared tin, and bake for 1 hour 10 minutes or until the cake feels firm and springy when touched. Leave to cool in the tin for 20 minutes, before transferring to a cooling rack.

Wet Nellie

"When I was a girl, my mother worked in a bakery and this recipe was their way of using up un-sold Madeira and sponge cakes at the end of the day. My mother never minded giving away this trade secret – but she'd never tell me why it was called Wet Nellie. Now we'll never know!"

Ingredients

8 oz (225 g) self-raising flour
4 oz (110 g) lard and margarine
Pinch of salt
Cold water to mix

Make up the pastry and line a shallow 7" square tin with half the pastry.

For the Filling

8 oz (225 g) cake crumbs
5 oz (150 g) mixed dried fruit (any combination) and
    candied peel.
1 tbsp lemon juice
4 level tbsp golden syrup (or jam)
4 tbsp milk
Caster sugar and milk to glaze

Method

Combine all the filling ingredients and spread in the lined tin. Brush the edges of the pastry and cover with the remaining half, pressing the edges firmly together. Glaze with a little milk and caster sugar and mark with a pastry cutter in a diamond pattern. Bake near the top of the over at Gas 5, 190°C, 375°F. When cold cut into fingers.

Banana Nut Loaf

"I say 'nuts' to bananas. They go together so well."

Ingredients

8 oz (225 g) self-raising flour and pinch of salt
2 oz (50 g) margarine
2 oz (50 g) caster sugar
2 oz (50 g) chopped walnuts
1 egg, beaten
1 tbsp golden syrup
3 bananas, mashed

Method

Sieve the flour and salt together. Rub in the margarine. Add the caster sugar and chopped walnuts. Mix beaten egg, syrup and bananas together, and add to the dry ingredients. Bake in a greased 1lb loaf tin for 1 hour. Gas 4 – 180°C, 350°F.

Note: Although this cake is usually eaten cold, sliced and buttered, it could be served hot, with custard as a sweet.

Christmas Cake

"Christmas Cakes come but once a year, and this is one to bring good cheer. Here's one I've made for many a year!"

Ingredients

12 oz (350 g) plain flour
1 tsp mixed spice
4 oz (110 g) ground almonds
4 eggs, size 3
5 fl oz (150 ml) milk or milk and brandy or rum
8 oz (225 g) butter
8 oz (225 g) soft dark brown sugar
1½ lb (675 g) mixed dried fruit
4 oz (110 g) glacé cherries – halved
4 oz (110 g) cut mixed peel

Method

Sieve together the flour, spice and ground almonds. Beat the eggs with the milk. Cream the butter and sugar together, stir in the flour and egg mixture alternately, a little at a time. Lastly, add the fruit, cherries and peel. Mix thoroughly. Grease and line a 9" round or 8" square tin. Preheat the oven to Gas 2 – 150°C, or 300°F. Put the cake mixture into the prepared tin and tie a double band of brown paper round the outside. Stand the tin on another layer of brown paper. Bake for 3½ to 4 hours. After 2 hours, put a piece of greaseproof paper over the cake. When cold, store wrapped in greaseproof paper and foil. Allow about 6 weeks to mature. During this time, I "feed" the cake with brandy once a week, but this is not strictly necessary. Decorate with almond paste (see page 150), and royal icing (see page 149).

Mincemeat Cake

"An excellent way to use up that extra jar of mincemeat after Christmas."

Ingredients

8 oz (225 g) self-raising flour
5 oz (150 g) margarine
5 oz (150 g) caster sugar
3 eggs
1 lb (450 g) mincemeat
1 oz (25 g) flaked almonds

Method

Cream the margarine and sugar together. Add the beaten eggs and flour alternatively. Stir in the mincemeat and mix well. Turn into a greased 8" cake tin, and sprinkle with the almonds. Bake in the centre of the oven for 1½ hours approximately at Gas 3 – 160°C, 325°F.

Golden Crispies

"Here's a dessert that needs no cooking. It's crunchy and crumbly, and not suitable for slimmers!"

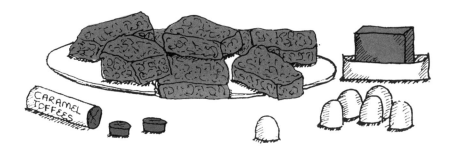

Ingredients

6 oz (150 g) crisped rice cereal
4 oz (110 g) butter
4 oz (110 g) Marshmallows
4 oz (110 g) Caramel Toffees

Method

Melt the butter, marshmallows and toffees over a low heat. DO NOT BOIL.

Stir in the crisped rice cereal, coating thoroughly, press into a greased, shallow tin and leave to set.

Seed Cake

"Seed cake used to be a popular teatime treat – try it out, it'll soon have you whistling for more."

Ingredients

8 oz (225 g) self-raising flour and pinch of salt
5 oz (125 g) butter or margarine
5 oz (125 g) caster sugar
3 eggs, size 3 beaten
1 oz (25 g) caraway seeds

Method

Cream the fat and sugar together until pale and creamy. Add the beaten eggs and flour alternately, beating well after each addition. Stir in the caraway seeds and mix well. Turn into a greased and base lined 7" cake tin. Bake in the centre of the oven for about 1¼ hours at Gas 4 – 180°C, 350°F.

Cherry Coconut Slices

"For a chewy, sticky treat try these tropical temptations! My family still love them and I'm sure yours will too!"

Ingredients

6 oz (150 g) cooking chocolate
2 oz (50 g) margarine
4 oz (110 g) caster sugar
4 oz (110 g) desiccated coconut
3 oz (75 g) chopped cherries
1 egg size 2, beaten

Method

Preheat the oven to Gas 4 – 180°C, 350°F.

Grease a shallow baking tray, or 7" shallow square tin.

Melt the chocolate in a basin over a pan of hot water. Pour into the tin and leave to set. Cream the margarine and sugar together, and add the beaten egg. Add the chopped cherries and coconut and mix well. Spread evenly over the chocolate. Bake for about 15 minutes or until golden-brown. Leave to cool before cutting into slices.

Sticky Chocolate Cake

"Chocolate cakes are always irresistible – and this one's no exception."

Ingredients

6 oz (150 g) self-raising flour
4 oz (110 g) margarine
4 oz (110 g) caster sugar
2 tbsp golden syrup
1 oz (25 g) cocoa
1 large egg, beaten
5 fl oz (150 ml) milk (approx.)
½ tsp bicarbonate of soda

Method

In a saucepan, melt the margarine, sugar and syrup. In a separate pan, scald the milk, and use a little of it to mix the cocoa and bicarbonate of soda. Mix all together in the first pan, and add the sieved flour, then beat in the egg. Divide into 2 greased 7" sandwich tins and bake for 25-30 minutes at Gas 5 – 190°C, 375°F. When cold, sandwich together with chocolate butter cream, and decorate with glacé icing, if liked. (See Icing Section).

Simnel Cake

"Traditionally an Easter cake with eleven balls of marzipan on top (one for each disciple, except Judas) – it's delicious at any time of the year."

Ingredients

6 oz (150 g) butter or margarine
6 oz (150 g) soft brown sugar
3 eggs, size 3, beaten
9 oz (225 g) self-raising flour and pinch of salt
1 lb (450 g) currants
4 oz (110 g) sultanas
2 oz (50 g) raisins
(or 1 lb 6 oz (600 g) mixed dried fruit in place of the
    currants, sultanas and raisins)
1 oz (25 g) glacé cherries, chopped
4 oz (110 g) mixed peel, chopped
½ tsp mixed spice
2 tbsp golden syrup
5 tbsp milk
1 lb (450 g) almond paste. (See page 150)
Apricot jam, and a little beaten egg to glaze.

Method

Heat the oven to Gas 4 – 180°C, 350°F and grease and line an 8" tin. Cream the fat and sugar until fluffy. Add the beaten eggs, a little at a time along with a little flour. Mix well. Stir in the spice, add syrup with a little milk and flour. Mix. Fold in the remaining flour and fruit. Place half the mixture into the tin and level. Divide the almond paste in half. Roll out one half into an 8" round and put on top of mixture. Cover with the remaining mixture, smooth level, and bake for 1 hour. Then reduce the heat to Gas 1 – 140°C, 275°F and bake for 2½ hours. When the cake is cold, divide the remaining almond paste in half. Roll out 1 half into 8" round, brush cake with apricot jam and place on top. Roll remaining paste into 11 small balls. Brush cake top with beaten egg, place the marzipan balls in position. Brush again with egg and place under medium grill to brown slightly.

Walnut Cake

"My Walnut Cake is so simple but oh so good – it never fails to impress."

Ingredients

6 oz (150 g) self-raising flour
4 oz (110 g) margarine
3 oz (75 g) caster sugar
1 tbsp golden syrup
2 eggs, size 3, beaten
2 oz (50 g) chopped walnuts
2 tbsp milk

Method

Cream the margarine, sugar and syrup together until creamy. Beat in the eggs with a little flour. Gradually add the remaining flour, nuts and milk. Put into a greased and base lined 7" cake tin. Bake for about 45 minutes at Gas 4 – 180°C, 350°F. When cold, cut in half and sandwich with vanilla butter cream, or fudge icing. Decorate the top with glacé icing, and walnut halves. (See Icing Section). This cake actually improves by freezing, but don't add the icings. Let it thaw out naturally and then add the fillings and decorations as liked.

Boiled Fruit Cake

"Fruit cake's a family favourite for Sunday afternoon tea. This one goes well with a cuppa any day of the week!"

Ingredients

Heat the oven to Gas 2, 150°C, 300°F. Grease a 7" cake tin.
12 oz (350 g) mixed dried fruit
4 oz (110 g) sugar (see Note)
4 oz (110 g) butter or margarine
10 fl oz (275 ml) water
1 egg, size 3, beaten
8 oz (225 g) self-raising flour

Method

Put the fruit, sugar, margarine, and water into a pan, and simmer slowly, covered for 20 minutes. Allow to cool. Add the beaten egg and stir in the flour, mixing thoroughly. Put into the prepared tin and bake for 1¼ hours.

Note: Caster sugar or even granulated sugar maybe used, but for a really rich taste use the good old-fashioned soft dark brown sugar. The difference is well worth the little extra cost.

Shortbread

"This is not only my own favourite but hugely popular with my family – even though she's now emigrated, my niece loves it so much I'm under strict instructions to make shortbread whenever she comes home for a visit."

Ingredients

12 oz (350 g) plain flour
8 oz (220 g) butter
4 oz (110 g) caster sugar

Method

Mix the flour and sugar in a bowl. Rub in the butter, cut into small pieces, and knead to a smooth paste.

For 'Petticoat Tails'. Roll out into two 7" rounds, mark into 8 sections and flute the edges.

Shortbread Fingers

Roll into a rectangle, cut into fingers and prick each with a fork. Bake at Gas 3 – 160°C, 325°F – for about 20-25 minutes or until pale golden.

Ginger Shortbread

Use soft light brown sugar instead of caster sugar. Add 1 teaspoon of powdered ginger to the flour. Add about 2 oz (50 g) crystalised ginger if you like it, and bake as above.

Note: Store in an air-tight container. Shortbread improves with keeping. In warm weather, chill the Shortbread before baking.

"The icing's on the cake ...
Or, if you're anything like I used to be, maybe it isn't ..."

"I have included the following section on icings and fillings – those most commonly used. I used to dread icing the Christmas Cake, usually managing to paint myself and surroundings in the process. Finally, I took an icing course at nightschool. We had an excellent teacher and eventually I mastered it.

There is one incident that I always remember: We had been asked to bring a good-sized rich fruit cake to decorate. I was working on the buses at that time, a split duty which didn't leave much time for baking. However, I managed to bake one, but it was late in the evening when it was done, so I left it to cool on a cake-rack and went to bed. When I came down next morning, to my horror I found that a large wedge had been cut from my cake, completely ruining it, for decorating. The culprit was my young brother, who had come in late, and said he simply couldn't resist it, as it smelled so good. I had to buy a cake, and make my excuses to my teacher. I don't think she believed me."

Icings and Fillings

Icing, like sauces, can intimidate the less-confident cooks amongst us. I used to be similarly daunted and had a few disasters but, after taking an icing course at nightschool, I became quite adept at this skill – although there were a few hiccups along the way. Don't be daunted, because in this case, practise makes perfect.

Butter-cream

Enough to sandwich a 7" cake:

Ingredients

2 oz (50 g) butter or margarine
4 oz (110 g) icing sugar
Flavouring and colouring as needed

Method

Cream the fat, add the icing sugar gradually, and beat until smooth. Add flavourings and colourings last of all.

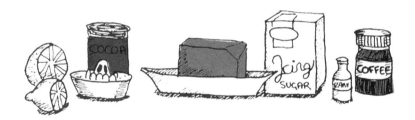

Variations

✓ A few drops of vanilla essence

✓ Finely grated lemon or orange rind plus 1 tsp lemon or orange juice.

✓ 2 tsp cocoa plus vanilla essence

✓ 2 tsp cocoa and 1 tsp strong black coffee (Mocha)

Fudge Icing

Ingredients

1 oz (25 g) butter or margarine
1 tbsp soft brown sugar
1 tbsp milk
2 tsp golden syrup or black treacle
4 oz (110 g) icing sugar

Method

Gently melt the fat, milk, sugar and syrup in a pan. Beat in the icing sugar. Pour into a bowl and allow to cool.

Glacé Icing

Enough for a 7" cake

Ingredients

4 oz (110 g) icing sugar, sieved
1 tsp warm water
Flavouring and colouring as required.

Method

Put the icing sugar into a bowl. Add the water and beat until smooth. Add flavourings or colourings last. Use immediately.

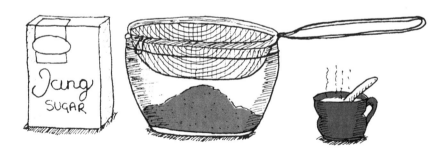

Royal Icing

Enough for an 8" or 9" cake
Ingredients

2 lb (900 g) icing sugar, sieved
5 egg whites
2 tsp lemon juice, for still icing or
2 tsp glycerine for soft icing.

Method

Beat the egg whites lightly, and add the lemon or glycerine.
Add the icing sugar gradually beating well with each addition,
and continue to beat until the icing stands up in stiff peaks.

Almond Paste

Enough for a 8" or 9" cake.
Ingredients

12 oz (350 g) ground almonds
6 oz (150 g) caster sugar
1 egg, beaten
Few drops of lemon juice
6 oz (150 g) icing sugar

Method

Put the dry ingredients into a bowl, mix well, then add just enough egg and lemon to make a pliable paste. Roll out to the desired size, using a little more icing sugar to do this. Brush the top of the cake with a little warmed apricot jam and put paste on top. Leave for 2-3 days to dry before decorating.

Preserving The Past

Great cooking is often passed down the generations and I learnt a lot from my mother as she did from hers. One thing I remember from my childhood is that mother always made use of anything to hand that was edible, and our garden was her inspiration. I hope you enjoy these recipes, as I have for longer than I can remember.

Elderflower Cooler

"Here are two recipes using elderflowers, the lovely white blossom which graces our English country lanes"

Ingredients
6 heads of elderflowers
2 tbsp white wine vinegar
1½ lb (675 g) sugar
2 lemons
1 gallon (4.5 litres) of water

Method
Pick the elderflowers with the sun full on them, if possible. Do not wash. Some of the green stalks may be removed. Put into a large bowl, or clean bucket, with the sugar, vinegar, rind and juice of lemons (no white pith) and add the water. Cover.

Leave for 48 hours. Strain and bottle. Cork firmly and lay the bottles on their sides. Leave for at least two weeks before drinking. If left for any length of time, the drink will mature until very like champagne.

I usually keep one bottle back until the following April, to be drunk on my birthday. Last year's bottle was full of bubbles, and popped its cork when opened.

Gooseberry Elderflower Jam

"Here's a good old country recipe. Grow your own gooseberries and give 'em a gorgeous home-grown treat."

Ingredients

Makes about 5½ lb (2.5kg)
3 lbs (1.3kg) gooseberries (a little under-ripe)
3 lbs (1.3kg) sugar
1 pint (570 ml) of water
6-8 heads of elderflowers (Do not wash)

Method

Top and tail the fruit. Rinse well and put into the pan with the water. Tie the elderflowers in a muslin bag and add to the pan. Bring to the boil and boil for 20 minutes. Mash the fruit as it softens and cook until pulpy. Remove the bag of elder-flowers and stir in the sugar. Cook over a gentle heat, stirring until the sugar has dissolved. Bring back to a full, rolling boil, and boil for about 15 minutes.

Test for setting.

When set, pot in clean, warm jars and cover. The addition of the elderflowers to the jam adds a lovely delicate flavour.

Note: There seems to be a difference of opinion as to whether the jam should be covered while still hot, or left to grow cold. I have always left it to become completely cold before covering.

Rhubarb and Ginger Jam

"This old country favourite is particularly nice with scones and cream. Perfect for afternoon tea."

Ingredients

Makes about 5lbs (2.3kg)
4lbs rhubarb (1.8kg)
¾ lb (350 g) cooking apples, peeled, coved and sliced.
1 pint (570 ml) of water
2 large lemons
3½ lb (1.6kg) sugar
2 oz (50 g) crystalised ginger, chopped

Method

Wipe the rhubarb, trim and cut in ¾" (2 cm) lengths. Put the pieces into a preserving pan, adding the apple slices and water. Add the grated rind and juice of the lemons and tie the lemon pips in a piece of muslin. Attach this to the handle of the pan, so that the pips are suspended in the jam. Simmer the fruit until tender, about 15-20 minutes. Remove the bag of pips, squeezing out the juice. Add the sugar and ginger and dissolve over a low heat. When melted, bring to the boil, (a full "rolling boil," ie. bubbling all over the surface). Boil until a set is obtained, usually 10-15 minutes. Test for a set, by removing the pan from heat and spoon a little jam onto a clean plate and cool it. Draw your finger through the jam and if it wrinkles it is ready. Pour into clean warm jars, cover and label. Store in a cool dark cupboard.

Rhubarb Chutney (Microwave)

"Rhubarb Chutney's perfect with cold dishes. And this makes a change from traditional tomato or new-fangled mango."

Ingredients

Makes 2-3 lbs (900g to 1.4kg)
1 lb rhubarb (450 g)
8 oz (225 g) onion peeled
8 oz (225 g) cooking apples, peeled
4 oz (110 g) soft, light-brown sugar
1 tsp ground allspice
1 tsp ground ginger
1 tsp mustard seeds, crushed (or level tsp of mustard)
10 fluid oz (275 ml) vinegar
4 oz (110 g) raisins

Method

Clean and trim the rhubarb, cut into 1" pieces. If you have a food processor, chop roughly the rhubarb, apple, onion and raisins together. If you have not, finely chop all above ingredients. Put all the ingredients into a large microwave dish. Cover and cook on High for 15-20 minutes, stirring at frequent intervals, until the mixture is thick and soft. Leave to stand for 5 minutes, then pour into clean, warm jars.

Cover and store for at least 4 weeks to allow the flavours to mature. Good with cold meats, cheese, or Ploughman's Lunch.

Golden Mincemeat

"This mincemeat is different from the traditional type, but it makes a lovely colourful and tasty filling for tarts and flans."

Ingredients

Makes about 6lbs (2.7kg)
3 lbs eating apples (1.3 kg)
½ oz (15 g) butter
2 lbs (900 g) sultanas
1 pint (570 ml) water
1 level tsp ground ginger
½ level tsp ground mace (or nutmeg)
1½ lb (675 g) sugar
4 oz (110 g) candied peel
Juice of 1 lemon

Method

Peel, core and slice the apples. Butter the bottom of a saucepan, put in the apples, sultanas and water and cook gently for 20 minutes. Add the spices, peel, sugar and juice. Heat gently until the sugar dissolves. Bring to the boil and cook for about 20 minutes, stirring frequently, until the mixture is thick.

Pour into clean warm jars, cover with waxed discs. When cold, cover.

Pear and Lemon Conserve

"Pick your pears early and you'll have a fruity conserve that'll last you through the winter!"

Ingredients

Makes 4 lbs (1.8kg)
4 lbs pears (1.8kg), preferably hard
2 lbs (900 g) sugar
2 lemons

Method

Peel the pears, quarter, and cut away cores. Put into a large bowl, add the sugar, mix well, cover and leave to stand overnight. Cut the lemons into small wedges, removing any pips. Put the pears, sugar and lemons into a preserving pan, and bring to the boil. Simmer gently for 2 hours, stirring occasionally with a wooden spoon. The pieces of pear should remain whole and the syrup become light pink and thick. A few drops of pink food colouring may be added.

Pour into clean warm jars, cover and label. Lovely as a filling for tarts, flans and sponge cakes, or as a topping on ice-cream.

Cucumber Relish

Ingredients

Makes 3 to 3½ lb (1.3 to 1.6kg)
1 large cucumber chopped – not peeled
1 lb (450 g) cooking apples, peeled, cored and chopped
1 lb (450 g) onions, peeled and chopped finely
8 oz (225 g) demerara sugar
1 oz (25 g) salt
½ tsp cayenne pepper
1 pint (570 ml) of vinegar

Method

Cut the cucumber into small dice. Boil the apple and sugar in the vinegar until the apple is tender. Leave to cool. Add the chopped onion and diced cucumber raw. Stir in the salt and pepper and mix well. Put into clean dry jars and cover. Leave for 1 month before eating.

This is especially good with cheese.

Index

Français

More of Mildred's tasty treats . . .

MILDRED SMITH'S TRADITIONAL RECIPES

This was Mildred's first cookery book, published in 1995 to accompany her slot on The Main Ingredient – and it's still going strong. It includes over 50 recipes with such old-time favourites as Lancashire hot-pot, cheese & onion pie and Bakewell pudding. The recipes were tested by staff and students at a local catering college, so you can be sure that the results will be absolutely delicious.

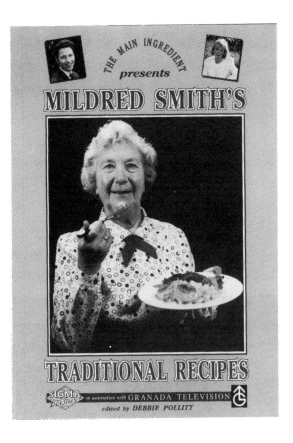

Available Through All Bookshops, £4.95

How to spend less time in the kitchen and more time enjoying your holiday!

Jean Smith's **"Caravan and Holiday Cookery"** is aimed at the four million caravanners in the United Kingdom, plus many more who take self catering holidays (under canvas, in mobile homes and apartments) each year both at home and abroad.

By cooking simply and using ready made items imaginatively, you can cook meals which are tasty, nutritious and quick to prepare! The meals have been developed over many years of caravanning – some were carefully thought out, some inspirational, and even some desperational, but all share one aspect - they can all be cooked on a maximum of two rings and a grill, using a minimum of utensils.

Around 130 recipes cover breakfasts, snacks, lunches, dinners, and barbecues; A brief UK regional food guide is included as a complement to the recipes, detailing regional delicacies and specialities.

The author, **Jean Smith**, has worked in the catering industry and has the benefit of the advice of her husband who is a highly experienced chef, working in varied environments from holiday camps to hotels, cafes to restaurants.

Available summer 1996: £6.95

MORE BOOKS FROM SIGMA LEISURE

We publish a wide range of books for North-West England
and further afield. Here is a small selection:

Eating, Drinking & Walking . . .

Seashore Sea Food: How to Catch it, Cook it and Prepare it!	£4.95
Teashop Walks in Cheshire	£6.95
Teashop Walks in the Peak District	£6.95
Teashop Walks in the Lake District	£6.95
Pub Walks in Lancashire	£6.95
Best Pub Walks in and around Manchester	£6.95
Best Pub Walks around Chester and the Dee Valley	£6.95
Pub Walks in the Lake District	£6.95

. . . or just walking!

Rambles in and around Manchester	£5.95
East Cheshire Walks	£5.95
West Cheshire Walks	£5.95
Peakland River Valley Walks	£7.95
50 Classic Walks in the Pennines	£8.95
100 Lake District Hill Walks	£7.95
Lakeland Walking: on the Level	£6.95
Lakeland Rocky Rambles	£9.95
Mostly Downhill (a series of three books covering the Lake District, White Peak and Dark Peak)	£6.95
Exploring Manchester	£6.95
Exploring Chester	£6.95

Cycling

50 Best Cycle Rides in Cheshire	£7.95
Cycling in the Lake District	£7.95
Cycle UK! The complete guide to leisure cycling	£9.95

Spooky Stories!

Supernatural Stockport	£5.95
Dark Tales of Old Cheshire	£6.95
Myths and Legends of East Cheshire	£5.95
Shadows: a Northern Investigation of the Unknown	£7.95

Local Heritage

Journey Through Lancashire	£7.95
Portrait of Manchester	£6.95
Portrait of Stockport	£6.95
Portrait of Warrington	£6.95
Great Days out in Manchester	£4.95
Reflections on Blackpool	£6.95
Reflections on Lancaster	£6.96
Reflections on Preston	£6.95
Liverpool Alehouses: including the Wirral	£6.95
Traditional Pubs of Old Lancashire	£7.95

Football & Golf

Red Fever!	£6.95
Despatches from Old Trafford	£6.95
United We Stood	£6.95
Manchester City: Moments to Remember	£9.95
Manchester City: an A-Z	£6.95
Golf Courses of Cheshire	£9.95

All of our books are available from your bookseller. In case of difficulty, or for our complete catalogue, please contact:

Sigma Leisure, 1 South Oak Lane, Wilmslow, Cheshire SK9 6AR. Tel: 01625-531035; Fax: 01625-536800

Cheques payable to SIGMA PRESS.
Major credit cards welcome